Beyond this Realm

Srishti Singh

This book is dedicated to my fleeting companion,

Mr. George Bernard Shaw's compositions, if I may be so extravagant as to call them mine.

"There are two tragedies in life. One is not to get your heart's desire. The other is to get it."

- Mr. Shaw.

~The quote which initiated my being to write, forever.

CONTENTS

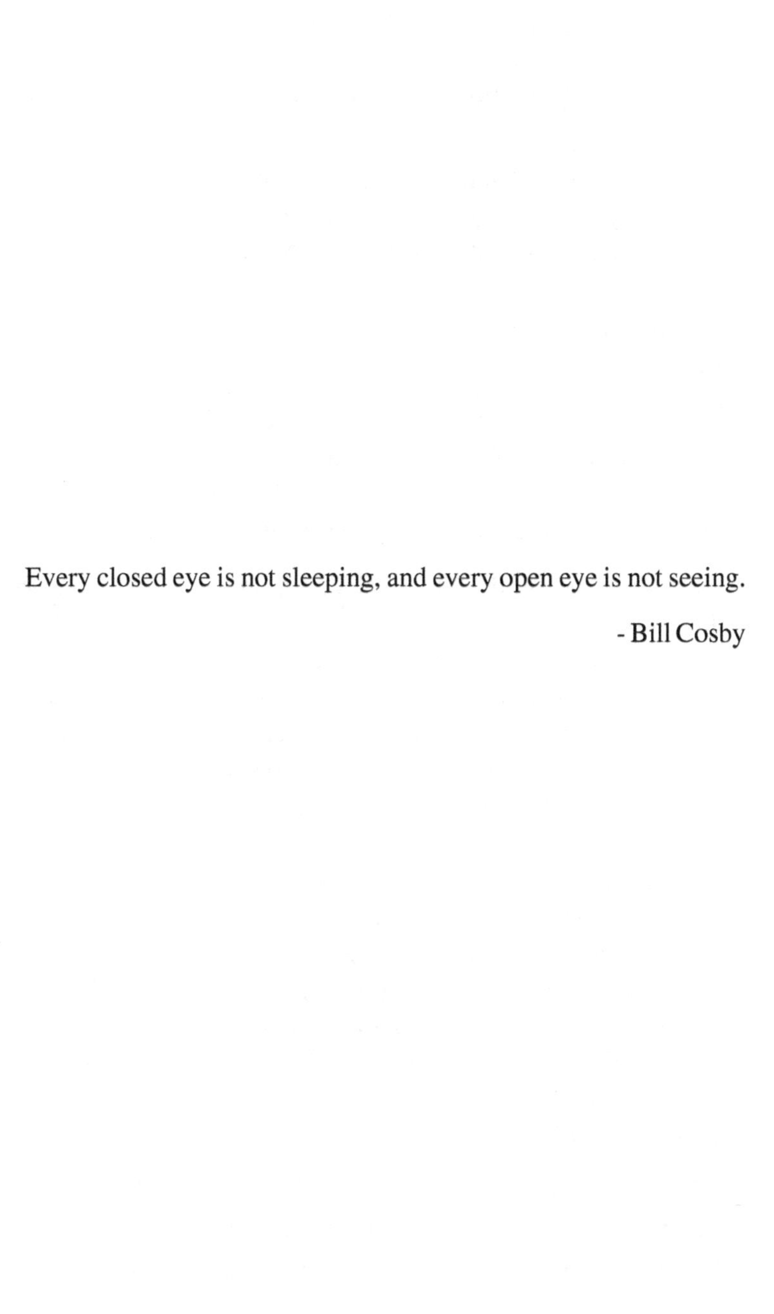

Every closed eye is not sleeping, and every open eye is not seeing.

- Bill Cosby

CALL OF THE HOMELAND

Walk with me, walk down the untamed path with me,
Call for me; call my name akin to the breath of the summer zephyr.
Flowing freely, disturbing calm, delivering penance to the
comfortable ones.
Let your voice cause tremors in the graves of the dead, and their
living son's.

Come, come alive in me. Your breath takes solace in mine.
Dig out the patriot in me; let your sane offspring's shine.
For the insane loath you, they are faithful no longer.
For the famous use you, they are indecently stronger.

Stake's rise in your downfall each day. Many are hooked onto that
dumb drug.
Aiding and abetting embezzlers abound,
Uprooting your foundation in broad daylight, without muffling sounds.
Make them crumble with your roar, let the crescendo unabashedly soar.
Take them; take the freedom they so frivolously exploit.
Make them; make them pay, trap them with a quoit.

We, who honor you, hold us tight and fumigate our fright.
Our love for you is purely blind.
We don't look deep, for the fear of what we might find.
Eradicate all our doubts so that we love you free.
Make us believe in your glory, force us to see.
For my countrymen and I, are blinded by self-induced haze,
Shake us awake; draw us out from this daze.
Remind us that we are Indians, living free in your wake.
Looting from our mother, leaving nothing for her to drape.

Call for us, call for all of us akin to the breath of a summer zephyr,
Let us save you before nothing is left of the Homeland in the fire.

I was within and without. Simultaneously enchanted and repelled by the inexhaustible variety of life.

-F. Scott Fitzgerald, *The Great Gatsby.*

CONTRAST

Life in all its glory beams at me. My eyes hurt from the stark contrast.
What is, and what could have been, are all exhibit in my twisted path.
I live in various dimensions, immense knowledge of all.
If one decision led to this, would other have beckoned my fall?

Life could have turned out totally surreal, I hang on to that mighty 'could'.
Writings of destiny are tough to maneuver, akin to engravings on wood.
Maddening monotonous patterns of each day swirl in my sight,
Clamping chains around my limbs diminish my might.

Seeing the future through fancy glass isn't exciting anymore,
The tranquility of life has eluded me, I pray for no encore.
Never too late to change lanes, than to shrivel and die in cowardice.
What is and could have been, shouldn't be a question for the wise.

At most the contrast would suffocate my being,
At least the variation would be worth seeing.
No doubt clouds the judgment, treading on an unknown path,
Frost would be proud, someone else imbibed his wrath.

For all to witness, I deviate from all I have ever known,
What is and could have been, no, longer rusts my lucid throne.

"Life is really simple, but we insist on making it complicated."

-Confucius

DELICIOUS AMBIGUITY

Delicious ambiguity of the human mind, breathes in the world,
Lives online.
Doesn't shake your hand when passes you by,
Tags you in a post, it reads, "FYI".
Oh, the birthday meets are so orthodox,
Who wants to get into good ole' talks?

Securing your home with a dozen locks, displaying your picture for
the world.
Oh my, what a cunning fox!
Trusting a GPS for directions to a loony bin,
God forbid enquiring of a real person, which would be a sin.

God bless the delusion of all mankind,
We love the technology and it cripples our mind.
Our heads are bowed; we are followers of the Android god.
We pray all day, fixated on his shrine.
Why care if the person next to us dies, our worship is divine.

Our lives are running on chargers, stocking up on battery destined
to explode.
Why meet people, why listen; why bother to talk?
Sit back, open a laptop and let's just stalk.
Our world doesn't need faces, hell it doesn't even need any sound.
Whatever you seek, whatever you desire,
The internet guarantees that it can be found!

 Put down the phone, look into the mirror,
You might just see a face you recognize.

Open the door, take the stairs,
Venture in the world, witness what lies outside.

Delicious ambiguity of the human mind,
Survives by killing brothers, believes its kind.
Screams, shouts, yells at the world to get better,
When asked to spell "communication';
Forgot the entire letter.
Raises voice for a day or two, when called for help;
Bids adieu.

Every saint has a past, every sinner has a future.

- Oscar Wilde

FLAMES

That undying desire to rise above this world.
This incessant chatter, fathomless existence;
The voice within straining to rise, untiringly persistent.
Poor excuse for lives; here the soul withers up and dies.
Ignorance claiming senses; hare-brained notions clouding lenses.

Restless minds set out in search of light,
Tolerating mundane worlds is beyond the fire's might.
Flames- spread within and without, burning,
Igniting conversations, maiming to fit in. Yet, yearning.
Yearning for identical sparks, hidden beneath years of rubble.
Searching for fiery desires, akin to rising above the world.

Unyielding to invites from the puerile cult,
That intellectual blossom, untouched, unloved.
Petty race this human one, sleeps through real life.
Wakes up at dusk, reckons it's lost and wails like a child.
Exists in the mist of nonsense, celebrates being dense.

Not falling in this trap are a few un-anchored souls,
Sailing about shores; searching for the truth by assuming false roles.
Existence necessitates this charade, survival craves the journey.
Someday, these souls will falter no more, someday they will find
their match.
Hope lays crackers, makes the flames stronger, unhinging the
brilliant mind's latch.
Until that dawn, until that final pawn, scorching lives will persist.
Rising will be the dream, though impossible it might seem.
We begin by burning down the mist.

I don't deserve a soul, yet I still have one. I know because it hurts."

-Douglas Coupland, *The Gum Thief*

INCARNATION

Life has a new beginning.
Peace has a new meaning.
Nirvana seeks itself today.
What is left of yesterday?

Nothing but silence encounters me.
My palm fills, winding up the sea.
Bright Sun soaks into my skin,
The valley begins to lighten up, too large to measure.
I might have to leave, but it's still a win.
Who gets to cry out of pleasure?

A new day, a new addiction.
This one's gonna stick.
Worries are miles apart, this life's not meant to be sick.
Leave me here, n I will live an eternity.
No matter if time runs out.
Time has always been a traitor,
Cheats like a fiddle spouse.

But I don't mind, letting it slip.
It's a reminder that I'm still alive.
Even death wont grant me this heaven,
No matter how hard I strive.
For others it's just a place, for me its incarnation.
Let the world speed up its pace, I have learned all my lessons.
It may be God's will, but now it's my way.
Nirvana sought itself today, what is left of yesterday?

I'd rather live with a good question than a bad answer.

-Aryeh Frimer.

INSOMNIA

What am I supposed to make of this night?
It should be calm, it should be quiet.
Wind chills my bones, the queer silence bothers me.
Isn't someone, somewhere, thinking about me?
The thought ridicules my being, I see myself smiling,
Sleep beneath my eyelids now, still piling.

The mirror is too bright. Or is it too late at night?
Did I see the moon? Or forgot about it too soon?
No matter what I ask, the answers elude me.
Mind is on a hold, all logics have fled.
Don't feel the calm night, distant noises sound close.
The airplane above, the highway, the suburb,
Nothing is too far. All closing in.
Barren roads, guards on patrol, a lone tree.
Isn't someone, somewhere, thinking about me?

They spoil every romance by trying to make it last forever.

-Oscar wilde

LOST IN YOU

Lure me into your soul, for you are a maze.
So that I won't ever, try and escape.
Nor would I flee or ask for freedom,
I will have you to get lost in, you'd b my prison.

A slave who serves, 'til death wins him over.
A saviour who shields his master, far or closer.
I'll b him and all that you want me to be.
You are my existence. No longer, is there a "me".
Lure me into yourself, for I love a maze.
So that I won't ever, try and escape.

Running all my life, I never could stay in a place.
I defied recognition; what was real and what was fake?
Grandiose speeches about life, earned curses on my behalf.
Faith-belief or wisdom-knowledge,
Which was my half?
Convicts, everybody who was ever born.
Accept it gaily, or you'd be left forlorn.
Sensibility is a crime. What is mankind left to do?
Is there anyone worthy enough, to look up to??

Answers never leapt out to greet me.
Doubt never lost contact, it did indeed seek me.
Raging with chagrin and temper, losing loved ones in the way.
I forbade emotions. Tears give you away.
Forsaken state, dejected spirits, a lonely soul was I.
That is when I found you; life seemed good enough to fly!!

Let me just thank you, for lighting up a dungeon.
Let me just live in you, the way you'd summon.
Lure me into your life, because mine has been a bloody maze.
So that I won't ever, try and escape.

You can do anything, but not everything.

-David Allen

ME AGAINST MYSELF

Woke up in the middle of night, the clock ticks 2 a.m.,
Looked around to see this retired life, wished it a belated encouragement.
The day runs by without a second to spare, if only I knew d art of holding time back.
Sleep is scarce and nightmares abundant, if only I cud buy dreams, I'd buy an entire pack.

What should I cherish? The tragedies that wrecked me, or the sins I possess?
Which is worse? Living death saintly or d Satan's lively caress?
My hold on ground is as weak as my soul.
I am sure I have conquered a kingdom, of despair and some hope.

Dawn smiles over my head. Is it a smile or smirk...?
I haven't slept d entire night n m not ready to wake up for work.
I wanna dream, find my way back to fantasy land.
Where sorrows are nonexistent n hope is resting in my hand.
Where each day doesn't beckon a struggle.
And each night doesn't reek of masked dread.
All d angels are blessing my soul and the demons are long dead.

Insomnia is my only friend, and also my best critic.
Gives me an insight into my real self, spares all the gimmicks.
This meaningless existence calls for nothing but death.
I pray to lord to grant me one, he patiently replies, "not yet".

What this destiny has in store for me will always be a mystery.
Belief can b bought and sold with just a little bit of treachery.
No matter how often I pray, I won't ever become a priest.
The tired and slouch soul in me won't rest, until it is pronounced a beast.

Softness is not weakness. It takes courage to stay delicate in a world this cruel.

-Beau Taplin, Shed your sharp edges

MELODY OF TEARS

Ever heard the enchanting melody of an unshed tear?
While dispensing of it in joy or simply fear?
Carrying with it the burden of untold stories,
Dying a slow death amidst treasured worries.
Swaying deftly towards its much anticipated end.
Stops, at each new bend. Hopes... every now and then.

Shredding its beauty to express ecstasy,
Screams for help, when survival becomes messy.
Sends out a message to the life existing all around,
Something's been lost, will it ever be found?

Raped souls, abused kids, terrorized families to economical kills,
Screeching in pain, losing hope, pleading mercy, desperate to elope.
Silent screams for the world to interpret,
Victims, hiding beneath cloaks of shame; waiting to be fed.
Fed with love, fed with acceptance.
A silent plea, not worth any man's reluctance.

Give way to the voice of the unheard; this is their method to com-
municate.
Give hope to the bashed and hurt, they .
Hear the enchanting melody of strong and weak tears alike,
Those which drift in the open, along with the one's that hide.
Stopping every now and then, on each new bend,
Waiting… for you to mend.

I shall look at you out of the corner of my eye, and you will say nothing. Words are the source of misunderstandings."

-Antoine de Saint-Exupéry

"MIDNIGHT MOONLIGHT"

Out of hundreds, it happnd this night.
It was dark with no need for light.
The moon shone above, with its mysterious half hidden smile.
It took all i had, not to jump up in delight.
The brew in my hand, felt as warm as d moon's steady gaze.
When i looked down, there it was again, the reflection of this
celestial left me amazed.

Moonlight danced in the dark brown liquid, like a dame in her
lover's embrace.
The marvellous bitter flavor in my mouth gave away to some weird
sweet taste.
No matter how much i try, it wont stop staring at me.
God's window in the sky, may be that is how he nevr lets anything
flee.

Clouds threaten to hide it, beneath a heavy dark cloak.
Bt it manages to look like a candle, peeking from under the smoke.
Any comparisons to the moon, have been an utter waste of time.
Nthing and no one can strike a chord, not like this wind chime.

Deprived of all the gleam and glare, we settle for dark barren nights.
Life is so flaccid, so fickle and terrified.
Its evrythn the moon is not, even though, try it might.
Passing through a labyrinth, we loose sight of the easy way.
Aint nothing constant, not even the moon can be ours to stay.

Dwell in its beauty, breathe the moonlight like air.
'Cz what you hold in your hand tonite,

come morow, it wont be there.
The aura around the moon, is much like our own.
Either admire it, or ignore it, it wil find a way to be known.

Its swaying around the sky, leaving a silver veil behind.
Glitters follow it arnd, much in a haphazard line.
There is a single star that clings to it all the while.
Not sure why it wont leave the moon, it probably is a lost child.

If hope had a symbol, it wud have been the moon.
Nothing too flashy, nothing too sharp. Just a big serene room.
Crossing over is what it has to do, and so do I.
So i will let it dance across its ballroom, whilst i say goodbye.

It is the mark of an educated mind to be able to entertain a thought without accepting it

-Aristotle.

MY ENQUIRERS

How can I let my enquirers know, about seeds I carry, looking for a place to sow?
No wonder I look wavered, my feet wobble on shaky terrain.
If someone demands my identity, am I to provide them with a name?
A name doesn't define me, neither does my clan.
A region I don't belong to, over the map I span.

Eluded answers, unattainable quest;
Wandering for ages, with faltered zest.
Native tongue or uprooted culture, I look around for some truth in them.
Descendants lay false claim to these,
Ignorance clouds shrouding their not so genuine memories.
Show me the land I hail from, and I shall call off this game.
The game of seeking clarity; for I feel alienated, yet again.
I stay quiet in a gathering, I am not of their community,
They talk to me about homeland,
I escape with tattered dignity.

I don't look for nirvana, as yet. I am materialistic.
Pleasures of the world are abundant, I am sometimes a philanthropist.
But it doesn't lure me, healing someone's pain doesn't cure me.
Detested crimes, criticized destiny, anguished lives and a little sympathy.
Gave them all I could, prayed too. Looked once again into their eyes,
 no relations anew.

Strikes with friends, Rage of unions, didn't leave anything behind,
not even the mutiny of billions.

Broke barricades and stomped on boards. Blood roared with the
mob's rage.
Then I wanted peace, followed a sage.
He didn't promise anything, respected him.
Promises are mere ways to be caged.
Now religion and rebellion are at war within me, dawn lurks like a
pale ghost I don't want to see.
Let the night swallow me and my doubts,
Roots can't be sowed in, after the tree is in the clouds.

But I won't stop looking, I will have my pick.
There is someplace safe &sound, waiting for my soul to click.
My enquirers will have to wait in the storm; the answers have eluded me,
But I won't mourn.
The beginning needs to be unearthed before the end,
I own this life; its mine, won't let it be known as something lent.

May you live every day of your life."

-Jonathan Swift

NIGHT'S HALO

It is not as silent as one would like it to be.
But its close enough.
A handful of harsh lights you might see.
Silly attempts to appear tough.

Street lamps canvas the road like cops during a parade.
The night is a bereaucrat they solemnly salute.
No mist blocks any path, its the lamps casting a halo like glow.
Say what you want tonight, mere halogens steal the show.

One just might miss it, fatigue winning the race back home.
Look a while in the rear view mirror, witness your personal beaming
throne.
Easy on the race now, gulp the silent night.
Supress the wild eagerness, to reach home tonight.

Walkers are busy chatting their life's worth.
Blissfully unaware of what eludes them.
Not that one would call them ignorant, simply impurities in a gem.

Sleeping city, sleeping roads, even the dogs appear to have slept.
Missing the washed beauty of the sky which just wept.
An engine roaring somewhere, a gate creaking open,
Every sound is magnified, albeit a little broken.
This night may mean the usual to people, just an ordinary one. The
final line to a day's tedious run.

Listen closely and u might hear serene music.
Observe closely and u might see dawn's magic.

Feast your eyes, feast your soul, u own the town for now.
Tomorrow is yet another day, yet another morn to bow.
You are one of the chosen one's,
Live these seconds, thereafter start anew.
This beauty is lost on all but a few.

A woman has to live her life, or live to repent not having lived it."

-D.H. Lawrence, *Lady Chatterley's Lover*

ON THE MOVE

Can't stay anywhere for too long.
Can't listen it always, be it a favorite song.
Can't bust my ass, on the same job every day.
I don't think of it as a sin, to have my own way.
Instability keeps me stable, moving keeps me sane.
I might love the house, but would love to be on the road again.

Same places, same people, oh God, the same aroma.
What is the fun in sticking around, when you can be a roamer??
Fancy parties, lovely evenings or those big bad bashes.
The infamous outings, where everyone talks in separate batches.
It might be entertaining for a while, until it's fresh and ripe!
But the routine won't do again, even if there's a brand new floor to wipe!

Changes are important, they better be deemed necessary.
Life is meant for living, why use it as an accessory?
Wages may increase, friends might leave.
Money could happen, affections might cease.
What if there is no substitute?
Who cares?
Life still looks resolute.

Pile up the money, stock up the dreams.
Something you count on, might never be what it seems.
Give them their own pedestal to mount on,
Take a separate, unfamiliar path until it beams.
Beams with the bruises, beams with the love.
Gleams with your sweat, shows that that you're tough.

Can the world stop you from being a nomad?
Can the mighty lord drop you from his beloved shack?
Let them all surface when they please,
Your name will be long gone by then from the lease.

Being on the move is a marvel, imbibing that lifestyle will take its toll.
Troubles that seem magnanimous now will fade once and for all.

You talk when you cease to be at peace with your thoughts.

- Khalil Gibran, *The Prophet*

NO LONGER NUMB

I opened my eyes to a new light,
For the first time I saw what the world was like.
It was pure, it was clean.
It was new, it was serene.
I saw two eyes full of love; shimmering with tears,
It was then, that I decided to let go of all my fears.

I grew up like any other kid around,
Who enjoyed every texture on a pebble if found.
But it was scary being all alone,
It was weird, being away from home.
Then someone just walked into my life,
It felt so good, it felt so right.

I was young, I was naive,
I was eager and thought I was brave.
Teenage years swept over me like a tide.
All I wanted was to fly free like a kite.
Freedom. Banishment. Mischief. Punishment.
I had it all, but it wasn't sufficient.
I wanted more, I wanted to live.
I fell in love, at least I thought I did.
It was confusing, it was tough.
It was driving me mad, but they called it love!!

I got over it, like every body does.
It's simpler these days. There is no fuss.

Then came life, the complicated type.
Rude, close, mean and loving.

All those faces that I couldn't wipe.
They taught me how to live, they taught me how to suffer.
They taught me what selfish meant, what people hid behind the cover.

I moved on with the carts full of ambition,
Rolled away and got a lot of recognition.
I was happy, wanted to stay that way.
Got married and was left with nothing to play.

Years later, I lie here, where it all began.
A hospital room, people who love me,
every one of those who possibly can.
I still remember those tear filled eyes and
the friend who came in my life.
Never did I forget the one's who betrayed me,
much to others dislike.
Haven't forgotten the punishments and
exhilaration of being young.
I can remember it all, feel it still, hell!

I AM NOT NUMB!!

I always wonder why birds stay in the same place when they can fly all over the world. Then I ask myself the same question.

ONE DAY, ONE DRIVE

Driving through the familiar lanes,
the picturesque landscape, taking away all my pains.
Its magic right before my eyes,
within the daily chaos, sanity shrewdly hides.
The noise of life doesn't bother me.
I don't really see anything beyond the breeze,
Sky opens up for me; my own heavenly abode.

Shades, hues, fallen leaves.
Crunch, beneath heavy laden feet.

Unmindful of beauty, steps continue their crunch.
Someone's making millions, lest begging for lunch.
The common ground where all rest, only platform where lives
aren't unfairly met,
sharing the same time earth, breathing the same air.

Ignore the sunshine like them, or awaken yourself with flair.

Pass the events by calling them miniscule, drift by life as a hazy mule.
Or rejoice in every step towards yourself,
Celebrate every plastic frame on your shelf.
Soak in the sun and the rains alike.
Walk out of gloom, stop narrating your plight.
Stop on your way, help a stranger or two.
The God's won't be blamed, they might thank you.

Close your eyes and listen, listen hard to your beating heart.
Match its rhythm to the music around, embezzle the world's sound.

No one will notice you swaying away; stop them to share your find.
Sing out loud, cause tremors in your wake, enlighten the sleepy
human kind.

Pry one eye open today, pray for it to pay the deed forward.
Don't stop now for the fear of being called crazy,
It's better than being labeled a coward.

The worst enemy to creativity is self doubt.

-Slyvia Plath

REGRETS

I should have known a lotta things,
But not all of them I know.
I should have been a lot more discreet,
but can't hide what I owe.
There should have been a lotta sense,
in everything around.
There should have been a gr8 flight,
before landing me on the ground.
I may live in regret,
this life that I have got.
Or I may just forget those blunders and consider an entire new lot.

"Give up or live up" is what someone once said.
I can't find anything to give,
so I'm just living up to my head.
Love, lust, happiness, all flies around me.
"take ur pick" it says, but I will just be me.
i'm happy without love, it might break me.
i'm happy without lust, it won't cure me.
I can seriously do without happiness, it manages to avoid me.
All I can'it give, is my life...
It is the one that looked out for me.

I won't regret anything that I did, I'm not naive.
Those mistakes were mine; at least that I can save.
I learnt from them and then I burnt them.
I saw them happy and then I cursed them.
I wanted companions, most of them left without a word.
Won't reveal names, some oath of secrecy I have sworn.

But I'm happy that I made something, even if they happen to be re-
grets...
They are my very own.
At last I can team up with someone and say "we".
Now I'm not alone, not like I used to be.

I made mistakes, and those mistakes...
made me...

To the man who only has a hammer, everything he encounters begins to look like a nail.

-Abraham Maslow

REWIND

Drugged out of my mind are the worries of tomorrow.
Why should I let the masked devil of fate scare me with promises so
hollow?
Why let the Satan decide what future should I borrow?
I will find the pearls, though few, in the ocean of sorrow.
I will rewind 2 the era where the mind refuses to let me go.
Because once there... will never reappear 2 face the chagrined blow.

Memories. Dreams. Prayers. And unkempt wishes...
The first of our several unexpected kisses.
When I was just about to kiss his cheek, the angel turned his face
And let our lips meet.
I melted in his arms, was at a loss of anything else to do.
It was early enough but I lost the bet. The only one i knew, was you.
Or I might rewind to the days when life was more than just nasty shit.
Because once I recall that... god knows I wont get rid of it.

To the moment when I found about other things than gravity,
Keeping me hooked to the earth.
All the feelings, luck, fate in my world, had little worth.
What kept me glued were the heavy burdens I never let loose.
The guilt I couldn't subside with booze.
The tears I gave away for the ones who owe me long deserved dues.
The joyous heart which pounded after hearing long awaited news.
But in the end came across the main link.
It wasn't gravity after all to throw me anywhere with just a wink.

It was the love that always pulled me down, lest I would have
vanished...
Never again to be found.

Destiny is now, playing games with me in the most lethal way.

I refuse to be caught so just tangled myself in the webs of yesterday.

Memories are where my loyalty is sworn.

They are beautiful... and probably the only beauty I have ever known.

So, don't blabber about a present or future & don't you mess with my mind.

I live in a world of my own, it operates only by a single command, "REWIND".

We don't meet people by accident, they are meant to cross our path for a reason.

-Anonymous

SATAN'S DOPPELGANGER

Oh, have I been wounded? Or just misled by my satanic mirror?
Do I strike the reflection in it or let my soul quiver??
Drenched in doubt, pinched with pain,
Detesting ignorance with emphasized passion, that's exactly what I
became.
Let the liquor wash over me, scant in quantity.
Little dosage, enough to shake reality.
I could see this world with just the right amount of indifference.
The crimes won't bother me much, nor would the sufferance.
Ignorance would come easy, anger over wrong muffled.
My haze will protect me from cruelty. All dimensions shuffled.
But wounds won't heal. Nor will the graves.
I was inebriated, but the world was awake!!
I was ruining my day; you could have done the same.
What you chose was pathetic, you inflicted pain.
So I'd drive again, drive my senses to a halt.
Kill humanity all you want, it won't be my fault.

Or, waking up might have been my calling,
Outstretched arms to prevent some wayward soul's falling.

Enlightened maze's with wise guiding posts, hidden glories which I
earlier explored.
Gave it all up for the pretense of indulging the self.
My God, What a stubborn stroke!
Sloshed nights, smoked lives,
hazy drives with abundant lies.
What I recall of them are poetic pigments, serene beauty and
musical segments!

What if I'd sketched? Dignified it as a memory, soul etched.
Wonder if I started writing? Wouldn't the picture be more enlightening??
Or if I was in control, knew every dice before it rolled?
If I had maintained my sanity, not indulged in vanity.

Done what I do best, held onto my ground, hell befall the rest.
Not letting my world swirl with hell's fury,
standing up strong, amid righteous jury.
Mighty is the Satan's Doppelganger, gives me a glimpse of bewitch-
ing madness.
Mirrors the devil in me with all its shrewd craftiness.

Free your soul, fly anew.
Kill the doppelgangers, bid them adieu.
Satan may still be on lookout, you be wise.
The world needs few heroes, pay heed to its cries.

A truth that's told with bad intent

Beats all the lies you can invent."

-William Blake, Auguries of Innocence

SHREWD SUCCESS

What do you live for when darkness prevails?
The tide soars, the storm rises and you set sail.
Waves crash in on your plans; all but nothing remain of your fans.
Soaked, wet, tired and bleary; life heads at you,
Leaves you weary.
Defenseless you stand amidst its attack,
Every blow leaves an eternal impact.
Like a hangover that just won't pass, obstacles turn you into a
sordid stagnant mass.

Do you have it in you? Are you one of those rare few?
Can you bear the storm and make it to the other side?
Would you rather let death claim you while you knowingly hide?
Make a point to make a stand.
Stand humbly erect even in creeping sand.
Sands of time might slowly sweep your feet away,
Whilst you rejoice in breathing, it initiates your decay.

Success shrewdly hides behind failures,
Are you too lazy to peel off the layers?
Weren't the wars of history declared in galore?
Fallen martyrs gave performances worth encore.
Stop leaning on crutches, made from your guilt.
Absolve your soul; drag your feet off the silt.

Blaming your weaknesses for epic falls,
Quit hiding behind them when your duty calls.
Overcome. Conquer. Wave a victory flag over them,

Don't let the tear(s) in your flag bother you.
Hardships bless the chosen few.

Has your response changed now? Is sweat still trickling off your bow?
Do you have it in you? Are you REALY one of those rare few?

Two things are infinite: the universe and human stupidity; and I'm not sure about the universe."

-Albert Einstein

STAY UP!

Jolts you awake from the embrace of slumber,
Success is enticing, failure; just a number.
Narrow your eyes against the storm; keep moving forward, break all norms.
The dawn bows at your feet, you beat it in rising up.
The night falls deep in sleep, you stay awake, your mind- shaping up.

For the path to glory is not yet a runway, It's a maze through varied terrains.
Pack your courage. Stock up your nerves,
Get ready for wounds in these wondrous games.
The sun won't shine on you, the angels won't guide you.
All that remains is tatters of weakened past,
They fly, they burn, and they turn to ash. Your past, never does last.
Make your future immortal, written with the blood you shed,
Give it your hue, crimson for when you bled.
Celebrate every bruise, knock out whatever that reeks of pain.
Every wound on your body, every scar on your faith, won't go in vain.

Tremors rise from your efforts, failure shirks away from your path.
What you do today, what do moving forward, is meant to last.
For the path to glory begins when you do, the maze turns into a highway,
Only if you turn from your irrelevant maze too.

Face the line of fire, only way to test your mettle.
Bear, bear it all, there has to be more. Don't just settle.
You were born fearless. Don't fret now, hang on to the ledge.
Stay hungry, stay raw and always, stay on the edge.

Without music, life would be a mistake."

-Friedrich Nietzsche, *Twilight of the Idols, Or, How to Philosophize With the Hammer*

SWAY

Smoothens your edges, gives your roughness subsidy.
Those rising and falling notes of a well memorized melody.
Enriching, blatant, soothing without patent,
The crescendo sears, vanishes fears.
Major and minor combine, burst into music oh so divine.

Rugged roads of life, destination(s) uncertain.
Doubt in every mind, shoulders drooping from the burden.
Ease the pain, let out a cry,
Sing along the lyrics, don't be shy.

A lullaby hovers in the backdrop of your mind,
Look deeper for treasures, cherish whatever you may find.
Lazy summer afternoons, picnics with families,
Which song did you sing, that reminded you of lilies?

Sleepy humid holidays, with your grandma humming,
Never was it decipherable, came with all the loving.
Memories, triggered by an old lost song,
Touch them anew, relive them for long.

Catch every fleeting note; it will lift your dull day.
Watch people bustling about, they don't have anything to say.
Envision them with music in your head,
Conjure them dancing, on the floor they have been lead.
Watch them talk, really talk with other humans.
Bustling will stop, no dragging feet with omens.
Wish them well; these lost, tired deaf lives,
There is a cure for them, restoring all their smiles.

One melody, one note, one beat and some hope.
Taken daily, as many times a day as possible,
Preferably with Paul Dresser's 'Rosie, sweet Rosabel'.

Magical yet subtle, calmness washes over you like a low rising tide,
In a crowd or alone, sync yourself with music, why hide?
For the world needs wonders,
Insignificant, invisible to the naked eye.
Anguish is abundant, stop figuring out why.
It will last, it will pass. It will end and begin.
Troubles will haunt you every day, might as well sing!

Sway, for a day. Let nothing else matter.
Everything fades away, meanwhile Move like Jagger!

"The easy confidence with which I know another man's religion is folly teaches me to suspect that my own is also."

-Mark Twain

THE DARKNESS

When your decisions mock at you, for being feeble n weak.
When this world is such a shock to you, you wait for your time to leave.
Contempt, envy, rage and greed.
Trying to use it all, but lose to some selfish need.
Everything is getting scary; the walls are closing on you.
The door you run for now, never used before, won't open for new.
Darkness, anxiety, gloom and fear
Lurk beneath your skin.
You'd ask for help if it were possible, but you don't have any kin.

Let this strange tide engross you, its pleasant to belong somewhere.
Never before did a disturbed soul attain nirvana anywhere.
Demons within rejoice to the prime.
The last of the angels, they wave goodbye.
No love, no compassion, no sign of life defined.
Why use wisdom as a defense when one can get away by a mere lie?
Wouldn't let this taken away. This urge to be mean and strong.
What is left of the world if you can't decide where you belong?

Choosing sides might leave you bereft of all strength,
Make your way, take to the sword, and drop that meek wrench.
Life won't come and knock, its singing a sweet sour song,
'til you decide, it fades away, leaving you with nowhere to belong.

Barren parchment, tired soul calls out for nectar.
Who cares if its blood or wine? Spare yourself that lecture.
The Darkness beckons, one and all.
Scream, Live, kill the weakness before you finally,
Fall.

We are addicted to our thoughts. We cannot change anything if we cannot change our thinking."

-Santosh Kalwar, *Quote Me Everyday*

THE HOOK

Beyond the realm of your imagination, is some cursed burden and agitation.
Clinging on every word you utter, is some hidden meaning you would cover with butter.
Some dreams that you won't talk about, some screams turbulent in your walls.
A name causing loads of pain, a calendar with crossed lane.
A street u may never cross a face synonym with your loss.
What I once discovered while reading a book,
Everybody has something hanging by their hook.

You accept, you decline. You drink it with your wine.
You hide it from the world, something once made you cross the line.
A lie or a confession. A secret or a temptation.
The walls are never strong enough to protect an act of sin.
A fear or an obsession. A face or a procession.
The prize is never glorious enough to boast a fair win.
The baggage is always there, just have a closer look.
Everybody hides, especially from the wise, whatever might be on the end of their hook.

Shaded past, tainted present, doubtful future and your soul to threaten.
Dreams that you banished, desires left famished.
Decisions you regret, situations you could have checked.
Family, friends, love, lust, betrayal or debt.
If only you were aware, sensible enough to face the scare
Life would have been easy, without any load 'til death.
Now that you know, don't pause the flow,

Take notice of every error in each hidden nook.
Die happy, die easy. With a light heart and nothing sleazy.
Leave with no worries and you are off the hook!

Fantasy is escapist, and that is its glory. If a soldier is imprisoned by the enemy, don't we consider it his duty to escape?. . .If we value the freedom of mind and soul, if we're partisans of liberty, then it's our plain duty to escape, and to take as many people with us as we can!

-J.R.R. Tolkien

TOMORROW NEVER COMES

All the nightmares & self cast curses, unlock yourself from your long lost urges.
Days and nights will come and go, that's the way it has always been.
Don't shrug away what your heart wants to follow because your days are
Yet unseen.
Ignore all caution, let the world criticize. Stay to witness your late rising sun.
Don't wait, don't break. It's your life at stake. Because,
TOMORROW NEVER COMES...

Close the dusty files, before you finally close your eyes. That's not what you will
Want to see in the end.
The struggle, the pain, all the losses and gain; are silly laws to make you bend.
You were born for something special and you damn well know it.
You are full of exquisite talent, then why just throw it?
If this isn't the life, the life you wanted. Save the soul from more burns...
'Cz baby, you aren't naive and you know it too well,
TOMORROW NEVER COMES...

The sky isn't as blue, the petals aren't as new. Make it yours,
 Embrace all flaws as the world isn't what it should have been.
Design it, make it a reflection. Without u it's still incomplete.
Nothing is perfect. Why are you trying so hard?
Hallucinations and anticipations will leave you a retard.
The dream must prolong into reality.
Rule the life you desire, Stop breathing this charity.
Risk the peace to a set of drums; because it ain't said in vain, it's all

but true...
 TOMORROW NEVER COMES...

Searching souls, dreading debts, trembling tempers and borrowed breaths.
We all owe God, just one death. Don't make yourself die more.
Try living up to the dream you once had. Don't give up on something you love,
Time never traces its way back.
Life isn't alone in the final race, mighty death also runs. And let's face it,
TOMORROW NEVER COMES...

You are only given one spark of madness. You musn't lose it.

-Robin Williams

WANDERING

Packed bags, torn maps, and unlimited cash the wallet lacks.
Fellow nomads accompany me, a journey with no finish line.
Explore more, imbibe more, true living has not been declared a crime.

Fancy cities make my insides recoil,
Towns of peace bless my dreams with visions.
Untamed paths are my treasure islands,
Contain me within walls and my insides sicken.

The barely moving bus on the hill slope,
The village off the beach, the temple in the woods.
The palace within the city, the fisherman and their boats.
The cries of kids biding us adieu,
All make up for a journal's life, intricately sewed.

Seeds of wanderlust sprout their roots deep,
Slowing, enticingly, the addiction seeps.
Gets under my skin, flows in my veins.
The pursuit of unknown empowers me, calls out my name.

We, who roam the streets, are not lost,
Lost are the one's caged within their minds.
Captive are the ones, who live in penthouses,
Free yet chained, tip toeing amid land mines.

Be a wanderer, be a traveler, and be the free, untamed seeker.
The answers are buried, dead with humanity, look deeper.
Ask the mountains, quiz the desert, and grill the islands for truth.
Life isn't static, doesn't halt. You think you should?

Pack your bags, don't bother about cash,
Memories way too precious to buy, anyway.
Join a caravan, lift the self-imposed ban,
Simply wander, the truth will find you on its own, someday.

They say you spend your entire life, rewriting the first poem you ever loved.

-Anonymous

WE, THE POETS

Rebellion to existence defies the will to live.
Worthiness to write, defines worthiness for life.
Hope to rise strengthens the stride, earlier mellow.
Decaying matter everybody, heading to rot, albeit slow.

Significant strokes of pen on paper, those syllables's woven together.
The rugged feel of raw imagination,
Rushing and stalling for the end, sweet emancipation.
Hooking up thoughts on the pen dangling by the bookmark,
Seeing clearly through vivid trance, even in dark.

Gifted, the entire genre of word lovers,
Can keep the world at bay without any troubles.
At peace, yet never static,
Dynamic thoughts blow their well in place covers.

No, we do not worship The Dark one,
Merely believe in its existence.
No, we do not shun the real life,
Simply fake blessed ignorance.

Knapsack, diary and an active mind,
Enough to sustain the human kind.
Survival for intellect surpasses the body,
Poetry lives on for centuries, sometimes foggy.
Lines the lobbies of great hotels,
Stands the test of time in public libraries.
Waiting to be touched, waiting for some soul to touch.
Keeping the contents intact to prove its worth,
Holding on to the leather binding, enabling its girth.

Let us dream, for we will create the future,
Future of the rustic bindings.
Let us rebel, for we will treasure the content,
Yellowed content of our findings.
We, the poets, let us exist, for we will keep interpreting,
Interpreting life, over centuries, with our writings.

The day the power of love overrules the love of power, the world will know peace.

- Mahatma Gandhi

WEARING YOU DOWN

When the moon peeks put of the clouds at night, while you are travel-
ling back home.
The exhaustion, anxiety, and weariness everything to which you are
prone.
That sliver of celestial does a waltz for misty eyes.
Dark, terrible, haunted secrets, it deftly pries.
No more than a mere reflection, plays tricks with vision.
Works magic on a dark mirror, ignites flares around with precision.

Haunting troubles you lugged the entire day, swiftly begin to fade
away.
Don't dig deeper for unhealed wounds. Let them all lay.
For tonight you can rest, your enemies are all at bay,
Look for a tremor in the wind, make it yours, and make it sway.

Search for sleep no more; sightings of pain are as rare as that of a
plover.
Lie back now, get rid of weariness, and welcome the embrace of your
lover.
Mundane, monotonous tasks mark your day,
Then your life, before you can help it.
The slouch in your step isn't here to stay only if dare to skip it.

For tonight forget about the morrow, there is nothing to bring you
sorrow.
Swim in the moonlit night, swim for the numbness you seek.
Spill out the venom you pour as you speak, the day dawns away,
So shall your speech.

Slumber, oh the devil's weapon is upon you.

Happiness s a habit.

-Anonymous

WHO'S GOT MY BACK??

I can't promise to stay with you, not now.
I can't let your trust be misused, not now.
When I look around, expectant faces stare back.
Some I let down, most I didn't.
Say what you may, this is my only sin.

A shoulder to cry on, a pat to carry on.
A tear that fell down.
I was always there.
A fear to share. A promise to care.
A decision gone wild. When u feel insecure like a child.
I was always there.
But when I need a caress, a relation that won't perish,
Who's got my back?

Listening for hours to soothe you down.
Making you smile, easing that frown.
Giving all I have for you and your sorrow.
But, if I need support, who's got my back tomorrow?

I didn't start the trend; the world got messed up for you.
You couldn't stand the evil, even though its nothing new.
Determined with your trust in me, you let all the vices free.
But if I need comfort, where do I flee?
Letting myself go is a habit I lack.
The important question now is Who's got my back?

Whether you live to be 50 or 100 makes no difference, if you made no difference in the world.

-Jarod Kintz, *Great Listener Series Mute Women*

YOUR KINGDOM AWAITS

Isn't the morning exceptionally blithesome today?
Doesn't the grass tickle your sole, under the pressure it gives away?
Ecstasy in the wind, mayhap?
Perhaps it's your own mind singing.
Some rare days are just pure joy, they begin without cringing.

Notice the air that you absently breathe,
Watch, for the first time the leaves leaving their home.
Active beneath your feet, even dead, they roam.
Sudden clouds wade across a clear sky,
Exceptional shapes, drawing out a child's cry.

Complaining mothers running after their kids, not yet tiring.
Balloons flying away, popsicle mishaps, secure embraces they end
up desiring.

Impatient sun looking for an escape,
Catch its every move, before it gets late.
Dawn to dusk, miracles are abound.
All you have to do is listen, for the recurring sound.

Claim this day, make every lost creek your own.
Every flutter by a butterfly, each ripple by a stone.
No disputes will arise, your claims will be truly certified.
Sweep in to rule your personal kingdom, no war's will break your reign.
Open your arms, embrace the offerings without any shame.

Reach out and touch the day, feel the night.
Everything they offer, is in your might.
Your subjects beckon you to grace the throne.
Put on nature's royal robe and you will never be alone.